Speed Reading:

A Complete Guide for Beginners Quick & Easy Tips to Increase Your Reading Speed, Increase Productivity and Improve Memory

Jake M. Johnson

© 2018

information contained within this document, including, but not limited to, —errors, omissions, or inaccuracies

About Jake M. Johnson

Jake Johnson is a practical psychologist who specializes in Neuro Linguistic Programming (NLP). He has been studying human psychology for more than 20 years and believes that understanding the human brain and human behavior is key to living a happy and successful life. He major influences include Eckhart Tolle and Tony Robbins.

Prior to his passion for NLP, Jake Johnson suffered severe depression. He lost his wife in a car accident and this put him in a downward spiral. Ever since recovering from depression, he is more than happy, raising his 2 beautiful children by himself, inspiring those around him

His passion is to help people enhance different aspects of their lives, but he believes this starts with understanding their own brain.

"We can do anything in this world. We just have to believe and put our mind towards it."

Table of Contents

Introduction

Reading is a way that many people slow down the fast paced world around them, so people think that reading has to equal being slow. This isn't the case. You can read quickly, and it's something you can actually learn. It isn't just a gift that you're born with. Everyone can learn to speed read. Reading can be difficult when you're expected to keep up with work, friends, schools, families and other activities. There's only so much time in the day, so getting everything done can be difficult.

If you're a slow reader, you're not alone. The average American can only read about 250 words a minute. It can take you even longer if you're trying to understand something important or comprehend something new. Too many people it can seem like you're wasting too much time, but that's where speed reading comes in handy. Speed reading is the ability to read quickly, sky rocketing to 350 words per minute or even more, while still retaining the information you need to. It can help you stay up to date with the news, propel through classes, or just learn new things by utilizing your time in a more efficient manner.

In this book you'll learn different techniques to improve your reading. It doesn't matter if you're a slow reader that wants to get faster, or someone who can read quickly and just wants to get faster. This book can help you to reach your goal. It may take work at first, but speed reading soon becomes second nature in no time at all!

When Not to Speed Read

Before you learn how to speed read, you need to realize you don't want to read like this in every situation. It's important to realize when speed reading will help you and when it will be a detriment. Here are a few documents that you shouldn't speed read.

Reading a Legal Document

Never scan or speed read through legal documents. Legal documents are binding contracts which need to be read thoroughly and slowly. Not to mention that for many people they are difficult to understand, so you need to work through them slowly to pick out key concepts and fully understand them. Though, since legal documents are often very long, it's often tempting to try to skim or scan them. Just remember that it's not wise, and take your time. Give yourself ample breaks between pages so that your comprehension doesn't suffer.

Instructions

You should never speed read through instructions because you may miss a few steps or something important in a step. This is particularly important when you're assembling objects or trying to work with electrical equipment. If you miss key elements when reading instructions it may result in a faulty item or you injuring yourself.

Literary Pieces

Older novels or poems should be read at a normal speed because they're often not easy to understand. You certainly wouldn't speed read through Darwin or Shakespeare. You'll want to read at a normal pace because you'll often come across words and phrases that aren't used in everyday language. To understand these words and phrases, you'll need to understand the context around them. This is why going slow is essential.

Letters

If you are receiving letters from people that are important to you, then you should never speed read through them. These are full of emotion, which you won't be able to understand if you're zooming through it. Emotion is not easy to comprehend when you're speed reading.

A Breakdown of Speed Reading

Reading opens up a whole new world of information to you. It allows you to learn new things, partake in different conversations, and just live a more well-rounded life. Though, for some people reading is a chore. It can take time to get through a book, and reading the news can be boring and hard to comprehend for others. It can be easy for some people to feel like they can't keep up to current events because of it, and other people feel like they simply don't have the time to dedicate to reading and gaining a better understanding if it takes less time to watch the news or videos.

Speed reading engages your same senses that normal reading does. However, you're learning to read more efficiently. You'll learn to skim and retain the important information out of your books, magazines, news articles or anything else. You don't have to actually read each and every word on the page. Traditionally, people read by reading one word at a time. People are taught to move from the left to the right across the page at this one word pace.

In theory, if you can recognize words faster you are able to read faster than another person. However, other research has found that you can read two or more words at a time, allowing you to jump ahead in a few glances. Some people can even read several words in a glance until they stumble upon a word they don't recognize. They can even expand their vision to read horizontally and vertically. These traits are exactly what speed reading teaches you as well as teaches you to expand on. You'll learn how to string words together, resulting in an increased speed.

For speed reading, you'll also need to learn how to turn off your inner voice. Sounding words out to understand them will drastically decrease your speed and slow you down. Focusing on the material is important for speed reading, so you'll also need to learn how to cut out the fluff and hone in on the material instead of concentrating on distractions. Keep in mind that learning to speed read will take time and patience. It's not easy to break old habits and throw out what you already know. You have to completely re-teach yourself how to read a book or article so that you can get to the speed you want.

The Benefits of Reading

Before you can understand the benefits of speed reading, you'll want to understand the benefits of reading in the first place. Reading does a lot for you, which you may be missing out on if you get easily frustrated or read slowly.

- **Helps Depression:** Reading can help take away from your boredom, the monotony of day to day life or even take away from your depression. Reading is an effortless and inexpensive activity that can help transport you to far off places. Books can both entertain you and educate you.

- **Mental Stimulation:** Reading can help to slow down Alzheimer's syndrome as well as Dementia. It can help to reverse the aging of your brain, keeping it healthy and young. Just like your body, you need to exercise your brain as well. Reading will help to activate the nerves, which is exactly what you need for mental clarity and a sharper wit.

- **Opens Communication:** Reading helps you to communicate with people despite national boundaries, social lines, cultures or class divisions. It allows you to know about people coming from different backgrounds that experienced different things in lie. You can do all of it from the comfort of your own room.

- **Personal Improvement:** Reading can improve your grammatical skills, spelling and your vocabulary. You'll encounter hundreds to thousands of words per day through reading, and many of them will be new. This allows you to learn different words through either looing them up or context clues. This will also help to enhance your grammatical skills and spelling. In turn this can help you to articulate better and express yourself.

- **Increased Knowledge:** This one may seem obvious, but you're expanding your knowledge with the more information you take in. it doesn't matter if you're reading fiction or nonfiction. You'll learn more about cultural influence, history, psychology, science, current events, philosophy or anything else you want to seek knowledge about.

- **Increased Creativity:** Reading can increase your creativity as well as your innovativeness. You'll be introducing a wide range of ideas and information to yourself, which will help to give you a fresh perspective. There are countless ideas out there, and by reading you're introduced to these ideas and can expand on them and create your own.

- **Increased Imagination:** This is the same reason that you'll find movies adapted from books to be disappointing. When reading you're imagining things in your own way, helping you too lose track of time. This helps to transport you somewhere else. This increase in imagination can help in other areas as well.

- **Enhanced Writing Skills:** With a developed vocabulary, increased grammatical proficiency, imagination, knowledge and creativity your writing skills will naturally be enhanced as well.

- **Better Concentration:** Reading can make it easier to drown out the world around you because it can be easy to get absorbed into what you're reading. In turn, this will lead to an easier time focusing and concentrating.

- **Overcome Biases:** You can overcome prejudices and biases by reading as well, since you're introduced to different ideas and lines of though which you normally wouldn't have. Opening your mind is the first step in helping to get past certain beliefs from your specific culture or society.

- **Enhanced Memory:** Memorizing a subject can be easy if you read about it enough and start to understand it thoroughly. When reading a fiction piece you're learning to remember the plot, the history, ambitions, nuances, characters, sub-plots and more, which in time will increase your memory. Non-fiction will help as well.

Speed Reading Benefits

You now know the benefits of reading in general, but speed reading comes with its own set of benefits too.

- **Empowerment:** Speed reading will empower you and sky rocket your confidence as you're more comfortable wherever you're going. Different knowledge is needed for different situations, and being able to gain knowledge quickly is freeing.
- **Money:** If you want to earn more money, speed reading can help. You can use it to get a degree faster and easier, take simple classes, or just do better in your job to secure a higher income.
- **Memory:** Speed reading doesn't just increase how fast you read, but it also increases your ability to retain the information around you. This can also help in other

aspects of your life, including your job, creative projects, and even school.

- **Lower Stress:** Reading can help to lower your stress levels, but speed reading can help even more. With more focus, more retention, and more productivity, there's simply less to stress about.

- **Problem Solving:** It's easier to solve problems when you have more information to take into consideration.

- **Fact Check:** It's easier to get your facts right when you can spend less time researching what they are. You'll feel empowered to learn more about a subject if it doesn't cost you too much of your precious time.

A Few Different Methods

Different people learn to speed read in different ways, and there are quite a few methods to choose from. Many people that learn will utilize a few different methods in order to achieve their speed reading goals.

Skimming

Skimming is one of the most common speed reading practices. Most everyone knows what skimming is even if they've never been able to successfully do so. It's a strategy that allows you to pick out specific details from what you're reading without reading each and every word. The reader isn't actively making an effort to read in a speedy manner, but it comes naturally when you glance through what you're reading to pick apart what is and isn't important.

Rapid Serial Visual Presentation

This is something that's used when you're using up to date digital reading system. One word will appear on the screen, helping you to focus on one word at a time, allowing you to take in the information in a quicker way. This is not what you'll use on a day to day basis.

Scanning:

This is another easy technique, but it works when you're looking for a specific piece of information in the material. However, with this technique you won't be reading the entire content. You'll have to comprehend what you can read and understand the material's structure before you can use this method.

Tim Ferris' Method:

This method allows people to read quickly by reading several lines in an immediate fashion by learning to enlarge your peripheral vision. It can be difficult if you have eyesight issues to begin with, such as you wear glasses or contacts. However, if you have good eyesight, this can be much easier.

Meta Guiding:

This technique is where you use a finger, pen or pointer, to direct your eyes to a particular word. This helps to reduce distraction, allowing you to concentrate on the words and enhance your pace. It's easier to follow a particular line, especially if you're struggling with comprehension, if you have a physical line guiding you.

Influencing Your Understanding

Speed reading will not help you to magically comprehend your content. You need to have a high comprehension level which may need to be worked on separately. Some studies suggest that someone can learn to read up to 1,000 words a minute, but you're likely not able to comprehend what you've read in that time. However, you can learn to read about half of that and understand it in a minute if you expand your comprehension as well. Going beyond 500 words a minute can be difficult because you have to move your eyes so that the fovea remains on the portion that you're trying to concentrate on. You'll not be able to distinguish you text outside of the fovea, which means you cannot process information if you read too quickly.

You'll also need to get rid of sub vocalization using speed reading methods, which include Rapid Serial Visual Presentation or even Meta guiding. Meta guiding is easier to understand, but both can be hard methods to use when you don't have a high comprehension level of the text. A main problem with Rapid Serial Visual Presentation is because you're likely to overload your working memory. If your reading speed surges too quickly, you may trade off with a lack of comprehension or general understanding. This is not always the case, but it's something you need to be weary of. When you concentrate on increasing your speed reading ability, move at a pace you're comfortable with. Pick out methods that are easier for you to follow, and always take a step back if you find that your understanding of the material is starting to suffer.

Training Your Eyes

Your eyes will need trained to speed read properly. If you master these techniques, then you will be able to master speed reading techniques too.

Eye Speed

Your eyes need to be trained to move quickly, which will translate to faster reading. You'll want to start with the numbers below.

2	1
4	3

You're going to want to move your eyes from the number one to the number four. Start with one, move to two, move to three, then to four. This will means you're making a z with your eyes before starting all over again.

3	1
4	2

Move your eyes from one, down to two, up and over to three, and then down to four.

Do both of these exercises ten to fifteen times per day. However, if you start to feel your eyes becoming tired or have pains in them, close them for a few seconds before you continue.

Expanding Your Peripheral

To speed read properly, you'll also need to expand your peripheral. This means you'll need to use a chunking technique. Start by focusing on the middle picture below, and don't remove your sight from it. Read the rest of the surrounding letters aloud.

B	N	T
R	☺	Q
I	U	S

Once you're able to read the letters aloud without moving your eyes from the smiley face, then you'll want to move on to the next grouping.

Bt	Nd	Tc
Ri	☺	Qp
ll	Ua	Se

Try to read the groupings aloud without having to move your eyes from the smiley face, and then you can move on to the exercise below.

	N	
B		T
R	☺	Q
I		S
	U	

Once you accomplish this, which will expand your peripheral a little more, then you can move onto the next exercise.

	Neil	
Bex		Travis
Rick	☺	Tom
Ilene		Sue
	Ursula	

Make sure that you practice a few days in a row even if you've mastered all of the exercises. You don't want to regress because you aren't practicing enough to keep your peripheral vision expanded.

Use Your Thumbs

You can use your thumbs to expand your vision as well. This will stretch your eye muscles to make sure that they're flexible and healthy. This will also move the muscles that are in your eye sockets in order to control your peripheral vision. Just stand or sit down while looking straight ahead. Stick out your thumbs and stretch your arms out to your sides. Move your eyes between your right and left thumb ten times. Do not move your head. Repeat three times. Do this at different times of the day so that you can get used to the motion.

Write with Your Eyes

If you really want to exercise your eyes, then you'll want to move them in a way that isn't related to normal seeing. By concentrating on a blank wall far away from you, you'll want to pretend to write your name or another word using your eyes on that wall. It should be a simple word to begin with. Move your eyes like you would a pointer, and visualize that you're writing. Change up the word each time so that you start moving your eyes in different ways. It will be hard at first, so take it slow. Remember that if your eyes hurt, then you need to take a minute before continuing or take a break before picking the exercise back up.

Use Hooded Eyes

Your eyes are going to need a time out occasionally, and that's where this exercise comes in handy. Close your eyes partially, focusing on the top of your eyelids. Try to keep them from shivering. As you focus on your eyelids, this will help to sooth your eyes. Next, look at an object that's far from you. Your eyes should still be partially closed. This will keep your eyes from shivering.

27

Squeeze Your Eyes

This is another exercise you can use to relax your eyes, and it'll increase oxygen and blood to both your eyes and face. This exercise should take about three minutes to complete. Inhale slowly and deeply, and then open your mouth and eyes as wide as you're able to. Stretch out all the muscles in your face at the same time. When you exhale, squeeze your eyes closed tightly, and at the same time squeeze the muscles in your face. This should include your face, neck, and jaw. You'll want to clench your jaw. Hold your breath, continuing to squeeze for thirty seconds. Repeat all the steps at least four times, and then either stop for now or at least take a short break.

Some More Exercises

There are even more exercises that you can do to start speed reading, making it a part of your daily routine. Remember that practice makes perfect, but you'll need patience as well. Speed reading is a skill, and it's not one that you develop overnight. You need to work towards it slowly and deliberately.

Alarm Clock Exercise

You'll want to get an interesting book or novel that you keep to the side so that it's only used for speed reading. You're going to get 'lost' in this material, so it needs to be something that truly interests you. Fiction is recommended. Next set the alarm clock to go off in twenty minutes. That's when you start speed reading, and you'll want to write down the number of pages you get through before the timer stops. The next step is to paraphrase the material out loud or write it down. At the next reading session, try to read faster to keep from plodding through the material. People often turn to reading slow when the material is easy, and you want to break this exercise. Compare your daily exercises to keep track of the progress you're making.

One Minute Exercise

You need to choose something small like an article, and you're going to read it silently for one minute. At the end of the minute, mark the line that you're on. Now you'll need to take a piece of paper and then write down important points that you can remember without looking back at your reading. Calculate your words per minute and write it on the same sheet of paper. Determine your comprehension by how much you feel you understood the article and what points you wrote down. Do this daily and chart your progress, which will push you to go further each time without sacrificing your comprehension.

3-2-1 Exercise

Choose an article to read silently for one minute like the exercise above. Mark the line you're on at the end of that sixty seconds. Write down important points just like in the previous exercise. Now go back and read the same text, but this time you'll want to give yourself two minutes. Add more important points to your comprehension sheet. After you've done this, go back and read it again for just one more minute. Add more important points to your sheet, and record your results daily so that you can compare.

Chunking Exercise

The point of this exercise is to stop stopping after each and every word. Instead of skipping individual single words, you'll lessen the number of times you stop. You'll be grouping words together, and it'll increase your comprehension of compound ideas. Therefore it'll help you to understand the meaning of a text while still reaching greater speeds. Look at the example paragraph below. Every time you see a slash, you're ending that word grouping. Learn to read the groupings instead of words one by one.

- If you really want to/ get your finances/ in order/then it's essential/ that you analyze/ your spending habits./Start by reviewing/your different checkbooks./ Then for a month/ jot down everything/that you spend money on,/ including fast food/and expensive coffee or tea./ Add everything up,/ including your day to day expenses./ You're likely to be surprised/ at how much you really spend./ Look back at it,/ and make any necessary adjustments./

Limiting Your Eye Strain from a Screen

When you're reading using your computer, tablet or phone, it's easy to cause your eyes to strain. This is where it's important to make sur that you have your settings set properly. Try these tips to make reading from a screen a lot easier.

Font Size & Type

If you are reading from a document, you can change the size and font type to make it easier to read. You're going to have a harder time reading cursive than you would something plain. Pick a font that is easier and quicker to read.

Fix Your Screen Contrast

Your screen should be clutter free and your background shouldn't contrast the text you're reading. If you're reading from a website that has a lot going on, then you're going to have a hard time speed reading. You're going to want to make sure that your background is easy to follow. Many online reading applications will let you change the background to a soothing color that doesn't distract you.

Utilize Screen Savers

You can get screensavers that are constantly active, which will help you to relax your eyes. When you need a break but don't know how to relax your mind to focus on the task, then screen savers can help!

Screen Position

You're also going to want to make sure that your screen is positioned properly so that it's easy to read. You should be a comfortable distance away, but it shouldn't be too far away that you have an issue. The tilt of your screen will also make a large different because it will make your light contrast differently, so make sure that you adjust your screen properly before you start to read. It's best to have your screen at least an arm's length away while keeping the font big enough to read. Smaller fonts will be harder to read, so you may need them closer if you can't adjust the font size.

Increasing Your Comprehension

You'll need to increase your compression if you want to use speed reading effectively, so in this chapter we'll be going over how to do that effectively. Your words per minute will mean nothing if you can't comprehend and retain the information that you're gathering from the material.

Use Self-Assessment

If you want to test your level of comprehension, you'll need to summarize the material you read. This requires that you assess what you did and didn't understand. Try to explain the concept of what you read in your own words, which will show you that you understood or didn't understand the subject completely. It'll get easier as time passes, but only through self-assessment can you tell if you're making any progress.

Push Your Limits

You'll want to test your comprehension levels through questionnaires, including crossword puzzles, connecting the dots, and more. By practicing compression tests, you'll be able to expand your speed reading capabilities from the comfort of your own home.

Enhancing Your Meta Cognition

Your meta cognition is your ability to think about thinking. It's used as a tool that will catch your thoughts when you aren't being logical or practical. This will help you to detach from your own thoughts to check to see if they're biased. It can also help stop sub-vocalization, which will help you to speed read.

Opening Your Mind

Reading extensively will help you to open your mind, and the more you read, the easier speed reading will become. You can only comprehend and expand your comprehension through extensive learning. Read about various subjects, and in turn that will automatically start to increase your comprehension speed. If you have a low comprehension speed, then you cannot expect to be able to speed read. You'll need to be able to quickly spot both similarities and differences between things.

Increase Communication

You should take your time out to speak to people that come from different cultural and socioeconomic backgrounds. Everyone has a different opinion, and you don't need to agree with it to learn something from their point of view. This is another way to increase your compression. It'll allow you to more easily start to see things from an author's point of view and therefore skim or scan a document easier.

Always Contemplate

It's also important to take the time to reflect on what you read. Turn the ideas inside out, and make sure that you explore them thoroughly. Speed reading gives you more time that you can do this, but it should not replace contemplation.

Stop Your Inner Voice

This is one of the hardest step to accomplish if you want to learn speed reading, but it's also one of the most important. When you're first learning to read, you learn that you need to sound out letters in order to read the word, which is called subvocalizing. This is a great way to learn when you don't know how to read, but it'll actually slow you down. This trait carries on with you through the years, so you'll need to turn off the voice in your head. Don't fear, you'll still be able to comprehend the words that you're reading when the voice is gone. There are different types of sub-vocalization that people use, and the first step to turning yours off is by learning which one you're using first.

Speaking Aloud vs. Internally

You have to figure out if you use an internal sub-vocalization, which is common, or if you speak your sub-vocalization out loud. If you are whispering or even moving your lips to mouth the words, then that is a type of speaking out loud. You will not be able to catch yourself subvocalizing if you aren't looking for the correct method that you've grown up using. Subvocalizing internally is the quicker of the two methods, so if you're a naturally quick reader, it's likely you use this method. However, it still wastes valuable time, especially when you're reading new material that might have words you're unfamiliar with. It's easy to get hung up on a word you don't know and then forget what you were reading, forcing you to start again. When you're moving your lips or whispering the words, you're essentially reading the text aloud, which will make you go slower. One of the easiest ways to break this method of sub-vocalization is to chew gum or have candy in your mouth to keep you from being able to perform the action.

Tips to Quit

It's no good knowing that sub-vocalization is hard to break, if you aren't given tips on how to stop. Here are some tips to help you quit subvocalizing as quickly as possible.

- **Your Hands:** You can use your hands to read. Focus more on moving through the words by moving your finger across the page. You can set the pace of reading with how fast your finger moves across the words, forcing your eyes to keep up with it. It can also help you to avoid fixating on reading or a specific work which will keep you at a steady pace.

- **Distractions:** It may seem counterproductive, but if you can focus more on something other than reading, it can be easier to speed read. There are a few ways that you can do this, including counting as you read. You should keep the counting simple, such as counting from one to three, so that you won't lose focus completely. Chewing gum, as stated before, can help. It can also help to watch something that you don't have to pay too much attention to or to listen to music as you read.

- **Use an App:** There are many apps out there that you can use for speed reading too. Many of these apps can be installed on the computer or on the phone, so you can practice speed reading anywhere. You can even set a pace, which can help you to reach your goals quicker. When choosing a pace, try to choose one that's at least 300 words per minute, since it's the optimal speed to get rid of sub vocalization without overwhelming you.

- **Force It:** You should force yourself to continue to read faster than you normally do. By forcing speed, you're having to focus more on the text. Pushing yourself a little more, can stop you from subvocalizing so that you can keep the pace you want.

Using Pacers

Now that you know what speed reading is and why you should learn, you can start picking methods that work best for you. The pacing method is the easiest to start with, but you may want to try a few different methods or even use a few of them together. Remember that different people learn differently, so no one method is perfect for everyone.

Cover It Up

This is another tool that you can use to help increase your speed. Simply cover up the words that you've already read through. If there is less on the page, then you're able to stay focused on the information you need a little easier. If there are a lot of subheadings, graphs, or just too many words on a page, it can be difficult to concentrate. It's easier to skip around the page, and it comes natural to reread information you've already gone over if you're struggling. It just isn't helpful.

After you've learned to successfully speed read and it becomes second nature, covering up the previous information often isn't necessary, but at the beginning it's much easier. You can't afford to waste time looking over things you've already read. So just grab a piece of paper, and cover the lines that you've read in order to keep a steady pace. By the end of the page, one page will be entirely covered so that you can move onto the next.

There are a few benefits to covering up your words. Obviously, you aren't able to look at anything you've already read and end up decreasing your words per minute. The other is that there is less distractions. It also helps to stop some of your sub-vocalization if your brain isn't try to remember past words. The paper can also be used to help push you along, driving you to go faster. If you know it's impossible to go back over words you've missed, you're going to try to comprehend the words quicker and recall them, helping to improve your memory.

Finger Placement

You can place your finger differently on the page, and different placements will work better for some people than others.

- **Left Pointer Pull:** This is where you curl every finger but your index finger. Place your pointer on the left side of the margin underneath the first line of words that you're going to start with. When you're ready to move on, move your finger down to the left margin of the next line.

- **Right Pointer Pull:** This is the same method except that your finger is on the right margin instead of the left. If your eyes come close to where your fingers are, then you know it's time to move to the next line.

- **Z Pattern:** This is a great method for newspapers and magazines, and start b pointing the index finger. Place your finger at the beginning of the line, starting by placing it on the left margin. Move your eyes to the right and rag your finger to the right while you do so. As you reach the end of the line, you'll need to drag your finger down diagonally a couple of lines, placing it at the left margin at the beginning of the line. Keep the finger there, trying to read as fast as you can to get to your finger. When you get to your finger, drag it to the right as you drag it down. Repeat until you finish the section you're trying to read.

- **Center Pointer Pull:** If you're reading something narrow such as a magazine or newspaper, you'll want to use this technique. Point your index finger, no matter which hand you're using, and then place the finger in the center under the line that you're going to read. Place it a few lines below, expanding your peripheral vision, and then move your eyes to the left as you move your finger down when you read. You need to make sure that your finger stays in the center.

- **S Pattern:** This technique is similar to the z pattern, but its uses curves. Point your index finger, and then place it under the line in the middle. Move your finger across the line as you read, and then move it down in a curving shape under the beginning of a new line. Continue to move your finger in an s pattern, which will encourage your eyes to move quickly.

Using Multiple Fingers

Some people prefer to use multiple fingers because it gives you more focus and control over what you're reading. Here are a few multiple finger techniques to choose from.

- **Long Underline:** You'll want to use this method if you're reading a wide column. Your fingers would be pulling your eyes in the direction you want them to go. Point your index, middle and ring finger together, making sure to pull your middle finger slightly back so that your fingers are the same length. Place the fingers under your line, and then as you read you'll need to move them towards the end of your line. Quickly move them to underneath the next line when you finish that one. It should look like you're jumping lines. Moving your fingers quickly means that you'll be forcing yourself to speed read.

- **Short Underline:** This is similar to the previous technique, but you don't go all the way with the short underline technique. Point your middle, index and ring finger together again. Place them a quarter of a line away from the beginning of your line. It should be right under the line you're starting with. Move your finger across the page, but stop a quarter from the end. Your fingers will move only across half of the line or the middle of the line. When your eyes meet your fingers, move your hand to the next line again. Move both your eyes and your fingers as fast as you can.

- **Double Pointer Pull:** Start by using the index fingers of both of your hands, and then place the left pointer underneath the beginning. The right index finger should be underneath the end of that line too. Start reading, moving your eyes as quickly as you can from your left to your right. Lower your pointer fingers down the line when you get to the end. Continue until you get to the end of your material.

- **Star Trek Method:** Also known as the Vulcan, this method uses the same hand gestures that Vulcans do in Star Trek. It's similar to the double pointing method, but you close your left hand making a fist. Point your index and pinky finger out. Place your index finger under the beginning of your line. Your pinky finger needs to be placed at the end of that line. Move your eyes from fingertip to fingertip, and then lower it to do the same to the next line.

- **Short Vulcan:** This is the same method, but instead of your pinky finger needs to be placed a third of the way down. This means that your fingers are placed in the center of your line. Move your eyes from the beginning of the line to your pinky finger, and then move your hand down. Continue until you finish the material.

- **Open Handed:** This can be used in both wide and narrow columns, but most people prefer to use it when they have a lot to read with wide columns. Open your hand, laying it over the text. Your middle finger should be in the center of your column. Make an S shape pattern with your hand as you wiggle it back and forth. Your hand should be resting comfortably as you move it down.

Using Cards

You already know the regular card or paper method where you place it over what you're reading, but there is also the card cutout method as well as other paces that you can use. Here are a few physical pacer methods that don't involve using your fingers.

- **Card Cut Out:** You'll want to use this method if you find that you're distracted by the text underneath your card or paper. You'll want to use regular white paper and then fold it in half. With a pencil, mark the beginning and end of the line on your paper. Also mark the height of each line. Cut out what you've marked, and place it over your lines. There should only be two lines exposed, and then you can read as quickly as you can, dragging the card down as you read the exposed lines. This will keep out distractions.

- **Ruler Pacing:** You'll want a transparent ruler when using this method. This will help you to expand your peripheral vision, and it'll help you to fixate only on the words written in the middle. Place the ruler in the middle of the text you're reading, and then use a pacer that will make you move your eyes down. Place it underneath the first line underneath the ruler. When you reach the end, then write down the words and word groups you remember. Repeat. This will help you to train your brain to be more organized, improving retention and concentration.

Advantages & Disadvantages

Here are some disadvantages and advantages of using pacers, also known as meta-guiding.

- **Advantage:** The main advantage is that you can read a complex text in less time. You'll swiftly run your finger through the text, or your pacer, which will force you to keep up with the speed you set for yourself. It also goes a long ways in eliminating sub-vocalization. Your brain will not be able to do two complex tasks at once, so you can eliminate the habit of sub-vocalization with this technique.

- **Disadvantage:** It will develop a habit of needing a meta-guide or pacer. You can also un your pacer across the page too quickly and force yourself to read without comprehending, which is what a lot of people do if they don't start slow and build up their pace. You have to find a balance for this technique to work properly. There will come a time when you don't need a pacer, and at that point it can hinder you to continue to use the pacer by decreasing your speed.

Reading First & Last

When it comes to reading something, you don't need to read every single word. There are some connecting words which can be easy to skip and still comprehend the material. Proper grammar may make it easier to read for some people, but it makes speed reading much more difficult. You can't skip over connecting words when you're talking, but when you're reading it's sometimes necessary. You'll need to teach yourself to skip words and you'll need to learn to pick out important words quickly. There will be times where you only have a few seconds to spend on the basics of a text before moving on to the next step in your project.

Even speed reading the whole text can become too time consuming in certain situations. Using this method, you'll still only get a basic summary of what the article or page is about, but it works better for what you need. For example, if you're reading a short chapter, read the basic introduction. Your basic introduction will give you a summary, but you'd get more depth if you keep reading. Once you read the summary, go to the final paragraph, or few paragraphs depending on how long the chapter is, and read those next. This will give you a summary at the end, which will go back over important ideas. If you go back to speed read the rest of the article or chapter, your mind is focused on learning more about the main summary parts.

The first and last paragraphs gave you an understanding and pointed out what you needed to learn so that you could skip past the fluff that wasn't necessary. When you come to a paragraph, don't try and read everything. Rea the first and last sentence to get a vague idea of what you'll learn in the paragraph. If it doesn't relate to the summary points, then just skip it. This paragraph isn't likely to be important.

The middle part of your paragraph isn't important because it explains further details, which often isn't necessary to understand a basic concept. While using this method, you'll want to also look at any graphs that are on the page or tables that are next to the text. These are usually highlighting important information that you'll want to commit to memory. If you're reading a textbook, there are often study questions at the back of a chapter or at the end of a particular section. This is another great tool if you're a beginner speed reader.

By looking at these, you'll have the questions you need to answer in mind. Alternatively, you may want to speed read through the text and then see how many of the questions you're able to answer. Don't get discouraged at first! You may have an issue answering a lot of them when you're just starting, but the more you practice at picking out important information, the more you'll be able to answer these questions through the art of speed reading.

Concentrate on Subheadings

It can take preparation before you can get started speed reading. It's a common misconception that you can just pick up a book and get a full understanding while speed reading right away. However, that's not always how it works. Most of the time you need to read the subheadings and do some prep word before you can begin.

Putting in some work in the beginning makes comprehension much easier while you keep up a speed you're comfortable with. By reading through the subheadings, you're able to piece together a basic summary of what you'll be reading about momentarily. This will help you to get into the right frame of mind to understand the text in as little time as possible. Your mind will start to form late questions from the subheadings, which you'll look for answers in the text. It will just take a few minutes to read the headings and subheadings, but it'll save you a lot more in the long run.

If you're reading fiction, scan for your chapter title or any bold or italics part that may be important. If you see something in a different language, see if there's a glossary to tell you what the translation is so that you have that knowledge before you read. However, reading headings and subheadings is a more effective way to speed read if you're reading a textbook or news article than a fiction story.

Skim the Text

This is one of the easiest methods for people to use when they're trying to speed read. It's a traditional method, and it's not too much of a jump. Skimming will let you get the essence of what the material is saying without having to read word for word. It all boils down to teaching yourself to pick out the most important parts without letting yourself miss aspects. To do this, you'll need to think about what questions you're trying to answer from the text beforehand.

If you're trying to learn something new, what is it that you're specifically looking for? For example, if it's a document for work, what do you need to learn from it in order to do your job? If it's a textbook, what do you need to answer the questions? If it's research for a paper, what part are you exactly writing on for your paper? How does the text correlate to that? Knowing the answers to these questions, means you'll pick out what you need to as you let your eyes glance over the page quickly. Skimming also requires you to read in a few different ways. You're not just reading horizontally, which is the traditional way to read text. You'll have to learn to move your eyes vertically to be successfully. Your eyes need to move quickly down the page to pick up speed. Knowing the author can also help you to skim something quicker. If you're skimming a textbook you've used a few times before, you already know how the author presents the information. They'll often use that same pattern in the rest of their work. You'll find that this is true for many authors. Not just in textbooks, but textbooks are the easiest to start seeing the pattern in.

When you know how the author argues or presents their point, then you can pick where your eyes need to go and pick out the information you need to retain quicker. No matter what, you'll usually find part of what you're looking for in the introduction. After all, not everyone reads the entire article or text. By putting their ideas at the beginner, you're getting a gist of what the author will present to you.

If you're reading a research paper or textbook, skim by skipping the proofs and examples. They're there to help you understand the ideas further, but they aren't there to present them to you in the first place. Don't bother reading the full sentence if you don't have to either. Not everyone has to read the full sentence to get a gist of what they need for it. Even if it's an important sentence, if you understand it from a few words, you should never feel the need to commit all of them to memory.

Skimming Checklist

When skimming here is a checklist of what you should pick up on. After you've finished skimming, make sure that you've did all of these things. If you did not, try again next time to be more thorough without sacrificing speed.

- **Title:** Reading the title is a must. Most authors will have important keywords in the title, and when you're used to looking for them they become easy to pick out.

- **First Paragraph:** You already know that reading the first paragraph is important. You should read it completely.
- **First Sentence:** The first sentence in every paragraph is important too so that you don't skip information that may be needed.
- **Subheadings:** You already know that reading subheadings is important, but you also need to try to connect the dots while reading these subheadings. This will help you to keep the relation that the subheadings have to what you're trying to find out clearly in your head.
- **Important Words:** You'll want to look at the actual text to find words that relate to the what, when, who, where, how and the why.
- **Qualifying Adjectives & Enumerations:** You'll want to look for these, such as best, most, least, and worst. These will denote important information you should keep track of.
- **Formatting:** You should look for formatting such as underlined words, italicized words or bold words. Bulletin points or numbered lists are often important to.
- **Last Paragraph:** Just like how the first paragraph is important, so is the last paragraph to finish connecting the dots.

Advantages & Disadvantages

There is always a time and place to skim or when to speed read through the entire text. Here's a look at the advantages and disadvantages of skimming.

- **Advantages:** It's easy to finish a text in a short amount of time with skimming, which is one of its biggest advantages. This is great if you have a test coming up and you need to study or brush up for it. It makes the perfect way to get down key points and central ideas.

- **Disadvantages:** People often fail to understand what skimming means, and therefore it is not an effective technique for most people. You cannot randomly pick a page and land on a spot before starting to read. Using the checklist for what you should and shouldn't be doing during skimming will make this disadvantage disappear. The other disadvantage is that if your eyes get tired, people will often try to push through it. You will need to rest your eyes when skimming or you will miss important information even with a checklist.

Scan the Text

You already know that scanning is a type of speed reading, but it's really a pattern of searching through a material. It's a skill you need in order to use in-depth speed reading. You're looking for either a main idea or a specific piece of information in the material without having to read each and every word.

What You Need

Here is what you need in order to scan properly.

- **Focus:** You need to stay focused and keep what you're looking for in mind as you glance over the material. Without focus or direction, your scanning will be pointless and you won't actually retain any information.
- **Imagine the Form:** You need to imagine what form the information will take in the material you're reading. What is most likely to be surrounding the information you're looking for? Are there particular words or headings that you'll find the information under? If you know this, then scanning can become easier.
- **Analyze:** If the material is lengthy or hard to comprehend, you may need to pair scanning and skimming. Skim the material before you scan it to map out what you need to pay attention to and what you can avoid.

- **Rapid Eye Movement:** move your eyes rapidly from left to right while scanning, quickly stopping only if you bump into words that may relate to the information you're looking for in the text. It's recommended to scan a page for about fifteen seconds. If it takes you longer, then you are no longer scanning. If you're experienced, you can usually scan a page in ten or twelve seconds. Scanning is usually done at around 1500 words a minute or more, but this isn't quite the same as speed reading since retention of information is only part of the goal.

Advantages vs. Disadvantages

Like with any exercise, there is both advantages and disadvantages with scanning something. there will always be a place and time for scanning a document as a part of your speed reading, but it shouldn't be used all the time every time.

- **Advantages:** The main advantage is that you can look for small data easily even if it's scattered through the text. You don't have to waste time reading each and every word to collect the data. You'll also be catching snippets of other information that is in the text, so you will get extra information as well.
- **Disadvantages:** This is a superficial form of reading. If you're looking for something as specific as names in a text, you may get the wrong names from the text. To help

solve this problem, you'd need to read a sentence or two before and after the information you find to make sure it is the right information. Otherwise, you may not pick out the correct data. You may have to read the entire thing if your information is scattered too liberally throughout the text, which means you'd actually waste more time and effort going back and forth. It's important to know when you should and shouldn't use scanning.

Read in Groups

You've learned to connect syllables in order to pronounce words, but doing this as an adult puts you at a disadvantage. Every word has a meaning in a sentence, but not every word is created equal in helping you to comprehend the text. Words in sentences will find partners that will form a word group, an alliance that helps you to recognize what it's trying to say. Recognizing word groups can boost your reading to reach 700 words per minute!

Take this example:
Your cabin in the Alps has a wonderful view that takes your breath away.

Now you need to divide it into meaningless clusters.

Your Cabin in

The Alps has a

Wonderful view

That takes

Your breath away

None of these words have true meaning when they're broken up into bad clusters. Breaking them up this way means that you'd need to read the entire sentence to understand it. Next, you'll see them broken up into meaningful clusters.

Your cabin

In the Alps

Has a wonderful view

That takes your breath away

These word groups actually mean something when you put them together. It can be compared to idioms. Idioms are a group of words that create a single meaning. They're a figure of speech which you're supposed to be able to recognize immediately without putting in the effort to interpret it. For example, when you say something is a piece of cake, you're saying that it's easy. By learning to read in word groups you're increasing your vision to keep your eyes from fixating and stopping. You'll improve your focus on the text, you'll easily be able to ignore filler words, and important verbs and nouns will start to pop out on you.

How to Start

Now that you know the concept, you need to know how you start.

- **Step 1:** Start small. When you're learning to read in groups, you may want to start with shorter sentences. You'll want to start with a sentence like: "The beautiful scenery meant more to him than he thought." Don't start with a sentence like: "When working with the new experiment, the scientists thought that it was best to differentiate between group A and group B, making group A the control group by providing them with a placebo." Which may be too long for you to break up in a glance without first practicing.

- **Step 2:** You're going to want to start with a pacer, even if you get rid of the pacer later. The best pacer to use is your index finger because you need to keep in mind the words that came before with this method. Remember that some people prefer to use a ruler, an index card, and a sheet of paper, or anything else that can move across the page with them. It really depends on you.

- **Step 3:** Review your comprehension skills. When you're practicing, you're going to need to take a step back to make sure you comprehended what you read. If you're slowing down to comprehend, you may be tired and need to take a break.

- **Step 4:** Set a time before starting the exercise. You can't just jump into speed reading for hours on end and make it work. Fifteen minutes is the recommended exercise time that won't burden the muscles in your eyes.

- **Step 5:** Delay judgement. There's no reason to judge yourself if you're whispering the words aloud from time to time. Remember that speed reading is a new skill that requires you to break old habits. Everyone knows that breaking old habits is anything but easy!

- **Step 6:** Now you can start to increase the time, but only when you start recognizing word groups. Your time is not what's important at first. If you don't have recognition of the groups down pat, then you can go quickly.

- **Step 7:** Keep practicing with breaks in between. Consistency is important. You should practice every day until you get it right!

Speed Reading In-Depth

If you're trying to learn something new that you'll need to apply later, then this is the best technique. However, it is one of the most difficult speed reading methods. You should go through the trouble of learning the slower speed reading techniques first so that this one is easier. This method is opposite of normal linear reading for studying, which is common.

The Main Steps

Here are the main steps to in-depth speed reading. We'll go over more of what they mean later in this chapter.

- **Gather Your Facts:** You have to gather facts from the text, cutting out the fluff.
- **Sort Them:** You'll need to sort the facts to look at if they're important or how they correlate between each other.
- **Measuring Them:** You'll measure your facts against the knowledge that you already have.
- **Selecting & Separating:** You have to separate the facts that you want to remember from the ones you don't care if you forget.

What Happens

Here's what happens when you try to use in depth speed reading.

- **Established Purpose:** You establish the purpose of what you're reading before you continue. Why do you want to read the material? How does the material benefit you? These are questions you need to answer before you begin.

- **Survey:** You're going to use the skimming or scanning techniques to survey the material. That's one of the reasons you learned them first! You may also want to do the subheading summary technique depending on how the text is set up. By surveying the material, you determine if you want to use it or not. Collect the main idea of the text so that you can determine if it's something you can benefit from.

- **In-Depth Studying:** Your main objective needs to stay in your mind the entire time. This requires focus, which is another reason you'll want to start with easier techniques. It can be hard to build up focus if you aren't used to speed reading yet. You're going to use the techniques you've learned up until this point to read as quickly as you can, especially grouping words together. Do not be afraid to skip receptive content or content that you find unimportant. That content will just slow you down. You need to keep in mind when, what, who, why, where and how when reading. This will help to keep a dialogue between you and the material, helping you to study. You may also want to make notes, jotting down what you think is important. A quicker way would be using colored pencils to underline important phrases or keywords. Use the method that works best for you.

- **Evaluation:** Once you're done speed reading through the text, then you have to organize your thoughts to finish comprehending the material. Comprehension is the main goal of speed reading, so make sure that all of your questions are answered. As much as regression can be bad for speed, you didn't do the exercise properly if you still have questions that need answered. So, you'll have to sacrifice speed to get those answers and just try again the next time.

Visualize the Words

If you're struggling to gain enough interest to read, then painting or visualizing the words can help you to get into a topic enough to focus on it. This will in turn help with speed. Pictures are much more powerful than words for many people, and that's why so many people struggle with a name but will remember someone's face. This can be applied to reading as well. It's easier to concentrate on something and grasp what the context means if you're visualizing it.

Test Your Abilities

Some people naturally visualize as they read, and others struggle with the concept. You should test for the ability before you go any further. Imaging hat you're laying down on a hill, looking up at the sky. Try to visualize the grass, hearing the birds chirp, and imagine watching the clouds drift over the sky. Imagine the grass rustling against you as the wind blows through the clearing. Was this hard for you? If so, then you may need to practice visualization before you go any further. You need to expand your imagination so that you can start to see something in your mind's eye without guidance. Then, it'll be easier to imagine something when you're guided by words. When you have this down pat, then you'll want to take a book or another reading material and put it in front of you. Remember that this is easier with fiction, so if you're struggling try picking up a fiction book. As soon as you read a sentence out loud, close your eyes. Try to conjure a picture of what you just read. Make sure that you're seeing in color, that shapes are clear, and even the distance that you're seeing at it. These details will become important later on. The more details you have, the easier it will be to comprehend things while you read.

If you've successfully been able to create pictures in your mind's eyes, then the next step is storing multiple pictures as you read. Challenge yourself to read three sentences to nine sentences at a time. More than that and it will be difficult at the beginning. Can you recall the details as you expand the picture? If you can, then you're starting to comprehend the material. When you exceed your mental capacity, then you'll start to lose the first and the last picture because what the words were trying to tell you will start to become fuzzy.

Content Isn't Equal

Some content will be harder to visualize than others. It'll be easier to read a fiction book and visualize it than a textbook, but if you can visualize what the text book is saying, you are still more likely to comprehend it. You will want to practice on fiction and nonfiction. Try expanding your visualization sessions to include books on animals, science such as basic chemistry, and even biology. Cell division is something that you can visualize! You don't want to get in the habit of just visualizing fiction alone.

Push Up vs. Push Down

There are two different exercises you can use when speed reading, which we've only briefly covered before. You're going to want to use both methods so that you don't get stuck. If you use only one method, you'll easily plateau at a low speed and be unable to move forward.

Push Down Exercise

When you're practicing this method, you're using the same material again and again. You already know the dangers of using this too much. You don't want to get used to the material. For example, you have an article on dog training in front of you. You take a section that is 500 words. You read it through the first time and it takes you 80 seconds. The second time, it takes you 70 seconds. The third time it may take you 65 seconds and so on. Now, each time you read it you'll want to answer the who, what, why, when, where and how questions. This will indicate your progress. The first time it may be hard, but it trains comprehension and focus.

Push Up Exercise:

Now let's pretend you still have that same article, and you took that one section previously. In this section, you'll take the whole article, reading it over and over again. You'll set the timer before you begin with this method. You'll start with the section you read before which took you eighty seconds. Now, the next time read that section and try to go further before the eighty seconds is up. You'll likely get into the next section even if just barley. Each time you try, try to push yourself to read further into the article in a short amount of time. This will demonstrate how much faster you're getting.

Be Aware of Eye Movement

You're going to want to be aware of your eye movement no matter what method you're using. In turn, you'll want to minimize how much you move your eyes when reading. Your eyes are used to backtracking when you're reading. Very few people can move their eyes naturally in a single fluid motion. Yet that single fluid motion is what will help them to pick up speed.

Keep your eyes as still as possible when reading, and always try to keep your eyes moving forward. Even when your head moves, you'll want to concentrate to keep your eyes still. It'll help you to focus on a single phrase.

If you're still having trouble, start moving your head from left to right while keeping your eyes focused and still. They should be centered and looking forward. Do not let them move with your head. This helps to establish a fluid eye motion. Next, you'll need to learn to keep your eyes moving straight without needing to move your head. Keep your head still, but keep your eyes looking from left to right. This will help you to speed read without too many movements. Keep in mind that your eyes and head are connected tightly, so practice will make perfect. No one masters it overnight.

Start the Clock

You can't be sure of the progress you're making unless you're timing yourself. You'll need to start by getting out something to read. You can either make sure you have a page and time yourself reading it from beginning to end or you can count the words on the page to get a more accurate assessment. Next, you'll need a timer. If you don't have one, you can usually find one on your phone, use the microwave, or even open up your computer and use one that's online.

Next, you'll need to write down your time, words per minute, or continue to use the same page. Setting a goal is also necessary. The best goal to start with is trying to reach 350 words per minute. Don't force yourself to continue. You once again have two options. Either force yourself to finish and see how long it takes you, always trying to meet your goal. Otherwise, you can just set your timer for a minute, and then stop reading. Count the words that you read in that minute, and continue to practice. Occasionally you'll need to throw in different material or you'll start to rehash information which will help you to go faster. This would create a false reading. Never use the same material more than three to four times.

Your true speed will be the words per minute you can read no matter what you're reading. If it varies slightly, which is natural, you'll need to take the average. Once you've mastered reading a page at a time, you'll have to also expand how much you're reading. It's important to push yourself to do speed reading sessions while keeping up your speed. Otherwise, you'll find that your stamina will go down. You have to teach yourself to focus for certain periods of time. Otherwise, you will not manage to learn to speed read for long periods of time. Just keep in mind that when your mind starts to wander, you don't want to push too much further past that point. Adding too much time at once can also be a detriment to comprehension, so you have to practice at your own pace.

Some Common Myths

There are a few common myths associated with speed reading that you need to get out of your head before continuing, especially if you've started practicing already! So many people think that speed reading is impossible, and it can be hard to believe that such simple strategies can have a real effect on the way you read. If you keep these myths in your head, then you're sabotaging yourself before you even begin.

No Enjoyment

So many people believe that you can't enjoy speed reading, but this simply isn't true. Many people actually enjoy speed reading because they're better readers. Reading goes from a waste of time for some people to something they can do quickly and effectively while understanding the material. When you truly understand the context of something, then it's easy to enjoy it.

It Takes Too Long to Learn

This is just a myth. While you will want to continue to work on your speed reading to reach new goals, you'll be able to learn how to start increasing your speed in only a week or two. You just have to be dedicated. On top of that, you'll find that while it takes time to learn, it'll save you time down the road. It won't take you years to learn to speed read, but most people will reach their highest goal in just a few months' time. You also shouldn't compare your speed to someone else's. Remember that everyone learns at a different speed, so you need to keep pacing yourself. Pushing yourself too hard will actually backfire and cause you to lose some of the progress you've already made.

It's All in the Eyes

Though you do need to move your eyes quickly in order to read quickly, moving your eyes too quickly over the page will simply set you back. You need to put your comprehension first while pushing yourself to move forward. Your eyes also can't move outlandishly around the page. You need to move your eyes according to the method you're using.

You'll Always Need a Guide

While keeping a pacer is important when you're beginning, you'll eventually outgrow it. Don't worry if it takes you too long. If you're having issues with the pacer or don't have it on you, then it's always a good time trying to keep your eyes moving and focusing properly without it. If you're concentrating on your speed and your eye movement, then you're less likely to count on the pacer itself.

Words are Skipped

You may not be concentrating on every word that you read, but you aren't actually skipping words when you're speed reading. Your eyes still need to go over the word and subconsciously take it in before moving on if you want to understand the text. Truly skipping words is not an option. If you're doing this, then your comprehension level will suffer, so you have to move over every word even if just briefly and without sub vocalization. You also won't be putting unnecessary words into memory, so that your mind is free to pick out what is and isn't important.

You Have to Practice Daily

While you do need to practice daily at the beginning, you'll eventually be able to stop practicing. Speed reading will become second nature, allowing you to use the skill when you need or want it without it being necessary to use every time you pick something up to read. You can still read the traditional way if you just want to slowly enjoy the material. It's completely up to you after you develop the initial skill.

Fingers are Necessary

While you can, and likely will, use your fingers to help you speed read at first, it is not a necessary habit to continue. Using your fingertips at the beginning will just help you to jumpstart your training, but it's a habit that's easy to break if your eyes are used to going over the material quickly. Not every speed reader will even use this technique at the beginning because it's about what you are or aren't comfortable with.

Some Supplemental Strategies

There are some non-reading strategies that you can use to increase your time as well, especially if you're just learning speed reading. When you pair these supplemental strategies with the reading exercises and speed reading strategies you already learned, your speed will take off in no time at all!

Your Reading Environment

Where you read will play a role in your ability to both comprehend the material as well as read in a timely manner. Having focus is one of the most important things you can do to increase your speed, so a place that has virtually no distractions will allow you to read faster than a busy place that's constantly pulling our attention away. You'll also need adequate lighting. If your lights are too low, you'll strain your eyes. This will make your eyes tired or even cause pain. Though, if the lighting is too soft it can be too relaxing. If you're too relaxed, you won't read well no less quickly.

A well-lit, quiet coffee shop is usually a great place to start. If you have big windows, then you're able to get natural light without it being too much too. If you're trying to read at night, then you might want to have a bulb slightly away from your head or at least a tube light, which many people think work better. If you have your light directly above you, you'll have an issue with shadows on your book. You should avoid places that are too bright, especially if they use fluorescent lighting.

Bright fluorescent lights can cause discomfort such as headaches, which will keep you at a slower pace. It can also damage your comprehension. Silence is another aspect of the ideal reading environment. If your reading place is noisy, then it'll be too distracting. Reading at home while everyone is away is quiet, and you can put on soft background music which will help to keep you relaxed enough to zone in on what you are doing. Some coffee shops are simply too noisy, so creating your own environment is a popular way to start speed reading. Noise tolerance is subjective, so you'll need to base what is or isn't too noisy on your personal preference and how easily distracted you are. A perfect reading environment should also allow you to be uninterrupted. If this is a concern, go to a place where it's harder for people to access you. A room that's dedicated to reading such as a study room is usually best. If you can dedicate a room at home, then you can customize it however you want. If not, most libraries will have study rooms that you can book in advance.

Focusing In

You can try speed reading technique after technique, but if you can't focus then it'll do you no good. Your ability to focus will depend partially on your environment, but it also depends on your mindset. Even if you have the perfect reading environment it can be hard to focus, especially if you have too much running through your head. An internal environment, such as your mindset, is also important to work on before you start.

There are a few ways that you can work on your mental focus. You need to identify what you do and don't have control over. Often, your distractions will come from worrying about something that you can't control. If you aren't able to influence the outcome of something, then you need to learn to let it go. It can be easier to dismiss worries when you realize there's literally nothing you can do to affect the outcome, allowing you to concentrate on something you can do.

Meditation exercises such as yoga can also help to train your mind to focus on the present so that you can focus on tasks such as reading easier. You just need to learn to be in the moment, which is easier said than done. For all intents and purposes, your mind is a muscle that you need to train if you want it to become function better. The Pomodoro technique is also a great technique for focus. It's where you focus for twenty-five minutes and then take a tive minutes break. This is considered to be a Pomodoro cycle. You'll need to do something else for that five minutes, such as play on your phone or just get up and stretch.

You need to rest away from the main task that you were doing, and make sure that you exercise discipline. Really stop when that twenty-five minutes is up, and then make sure you take a full five minute break without it lasting longer. It doesn't matter how enjoyable the reading material is. This will prevent your mind from getting tired too quickly, which will extend your productivity and time that you can focus. It's similar to a run-walk-run method when you're trying to train for endurance running. You rest before you get to the point of mental fatigue so that you can keep going.

Exercise Helps!

Many studies have shown that exercise can help your brain to focus for longer, so exercise can actually help your speed reading too. Exercising a few hours before you sit down to a speed reading session can help you to focus mentally. It can also help with reading comprehension because energizing your brain can help to improve your memory. If you don't retain what you're reading, then speed reading is a useless endeavor. By exercising regularly you're also able to release pent up energy that can make you fidgety when you're trying to read, which in turn will take away from your ability to focus.

Foods: Good & Bad

Eating the right foods is important when you're trying to build up your focus and retention. Nutrients play an important role in keeping your brain healthy and working optimally. You need to take a serious look at your diet if you're trying to improve your comprehension and reading speed. Junk food is a detriment to speed reading because it produces hyperactivity. Too much sugar will make you hyper, preventing concentration and focus when you're trying to focus on your speed and retention. It can also cause a crash and burn. If your blood sugar spikes quickly, which it often will when you consume junk food, your pancreas will release more insulin. Your blood sugar then crashes, and you'll feel drowsiness and lethargic. This will also make it hard to concentrate on what you're reading.

Surprisingly, tuna is bad for your brain as well. If eaten excessively, it'll actually keep you from focusing because you'll be running the risk of ingesting too much mercury. There are many omega-3 filled alternative such as trout, salmon and even anchovies. Another food you should minimize is ice cream because there is next to no nutritional value and it's full of sugar. Once again, sugar will spike your blood sugars, which will just lead to a crash and burn. Diet soda can also harm your productivity because of aspartame, which is known to cause problems with memory. You may not get a sugar crash with diet soda, but having issues recalling what you read is just as bad if not worse!

Blueberries top the list for good foods that will help elevate memory and increase your concentration even five hours after consumption. They have a large amount of antioxidants which will promote blood flow to the brain, which will enhance your speed reading performance. They also help to provide you with energy without inducing hyperactivity.

Another nutritional superhero is green tea. It gives you a mental boost because of the l'theanine and caffeine. Most people already know that caffeine is great for improving mental performance and focus. Le'theanine is an ingredient that helps to release caffeine slowly without just dumping it in your system at once. If caffeine is processed all at once you'll risk a caffeine crash or lethargy because of the drop of caffeine levels in your blood. L'theanine will help you to feel a little more tranquil while staying alert, which is a good state to be in when speed reading. Fatty fish, as we mentioned early, are great for staving off mood swings, fatigue and memory decline. They'll also help with your mood and your ability to concentrate. Of course, it's biter to bake your fish rather than fry them to avoid unhealthy fats and oils. On top of eating the right foods, you need to stay hydrated as well. Most people actually suffer from slight dehydration which will negatively affect your focus and concentration. Your brain gets the necessary electrical energy for functioning at optimal levels form staying hydrated. This includes thought activities such as reading and your memory, which means you need to stay hydrated. Staying properly hydrated also helps think clearly and faster. If you don't' like the taste of normal water, you can prepare fruit-infused water in advance. This will not only hydrate you, but it'll also increase your nutritional Dark chocolates are also a great food for speed reading because they aren't laden with sugar. They contain some caffeine and magnesium which can help you to handle stress. Dark chocolate also helps your body to release endorphins and serotonin, which will help to improve your mood and keep you calm. Keep in mind, this doesn't mean that you should consume an excessive amount of dark chocolate. Consuming too much of anything will be more of a detriment to your speed reading than a help.

Supplements to Help

If you don't want to change up your diet, you can take some supplement stop help your mental focus and improve your speed reading. These supplements help to benefit your brain. Just follow the dosage on the supplements that you buy. However, always make sure that you speak with our doctor before adding any supplement into your daily routine.

- **Shankpushpi:** This is an Indian herb, and it's mentioned in Ayurvedic texts. It's regularly consumed in order to sharpen your mind and improve your memory. You'll mostly find this in syrup form, and you're likely to only find it online. Though some health stores do carry it depending on where you live.
- **Rhodiola:** This is a root that's great at staving off memory loss, and it'll help to improve your mind's capacity. You'd need to regularly consume it in its supplement form, but it can help you with speed reading. You can purchase it either in a powder or in capsule form.

- **Gingko:** Also known as gingko biloba is a popular herb, and it's known in Chinese medicine as a popular way to increase brainpower. It's also meant to help boost mental capacity.

- **Ashwagandha:** This is an herb used in Asian countries, and it will improve memory and increase your comprehension. You can usually get it in powder or capsule form, but capsules are often easier to find.

- **Sage:** Sage extract will help to boost your memory, but you can also add a little bit into your meals. Still, sage capsules are a great way to get this memory boosting herb into your daily routine.

- **Turmeric:** This is another herb that you can cook with, but you can also find it in capsule form.it prevents oxidative damage in your brain.

Get Enough Sleep

All the mental exercises, dietary changes, and supplements you take wont' matter at all if you can't get adequate sleep. Your brain needs sleep to function properly. Without it, your speed and comprehension will suffer. Your brain needs time to recuperate, so if you feel lethargic or even weak when you wake up in the morning, you're probably not getting the sleep you need. When you wake up you should feel alert, refreshed and energetic. This will help you to focus during the day, especially when it comes to reading. It's more than just the number of hours you get in a night too. Your quality of sleep makes a different too. You can sleep for ten hours a day, but it isn't enough if you aren't sleeping well. If you sleep well enough, or deep enough, then sleeping six hours can still give you all of the rest that you need.

Tips for Quality Sleep

Quality sleep is easier said than done, so it might be best to try these tips for a better night's rest.

- **Avoid Exercise:** While it's good to exercise, you don't want to do it too close to bedtime. This will increase your body temperature, which will make it difficult to sleep. You shouldn't exercise three hours before you go to bed so that you have time to cool down and for your heart rate to normalize.

- **Turn Off the Gadgets:** You should turn off all gadgets and electronics a half hour before going to bed. When you expose yourself to artificial light, such as from your tablet, TV or phone, then you suppress the natural release of melatonin. Melatonin is an important hormone for sleep.

- **Cut Down the Caffeine:** Having caffeine too close to bedtime you'll still have it in your system when you go to bed. This will make you restless. You should limit your coffee take after three p.m. if you get up around eight or nine a.m. so that you don't have this issue.

- **Try to Relax:** It's important that you give yourself some time to relax your body and your mind before bed. Otherwise, it'll make it harder to sleep. Do something that doesn't require you to exert effort or stimulate your mind before bed.

- **Aromas Matter:** You shouldn't burn a candle while you sleep, but you can diffuse some essential oils or rub some on your pillow before you go to bed. Lavender sachets in your pillow can also help as well. Just make sure that you're using a natural fragrance that is relaxing, such as chamomile, rose, jasmine or lavender.

- **Cool Temperatures:** It's best to maintain a cool temperature when you're trying to sleep. Around 65 to 70 degrees Fahrenheit is an optimal temperature for sleeping soundly.

Conclusion

Now you know everything you need to know in order to start speed reading through fiction and nonfiction. Remember that it won't happen overnight, but you don't have to worry about how long it takes you as long as you're practicing on a regular basis. Practice your eye exercises and track your progress to make sure that you continue to move forward, but don't overexert yourself. Not everyone will pick up speed reading in a week. Everyone has a comfortable pace that they learn out, and all you need to do is find yours and keep practicing. Soon enough you'll be speed reading in no time at all!

29250609R00050

Printed in Great Britain
by Amazon